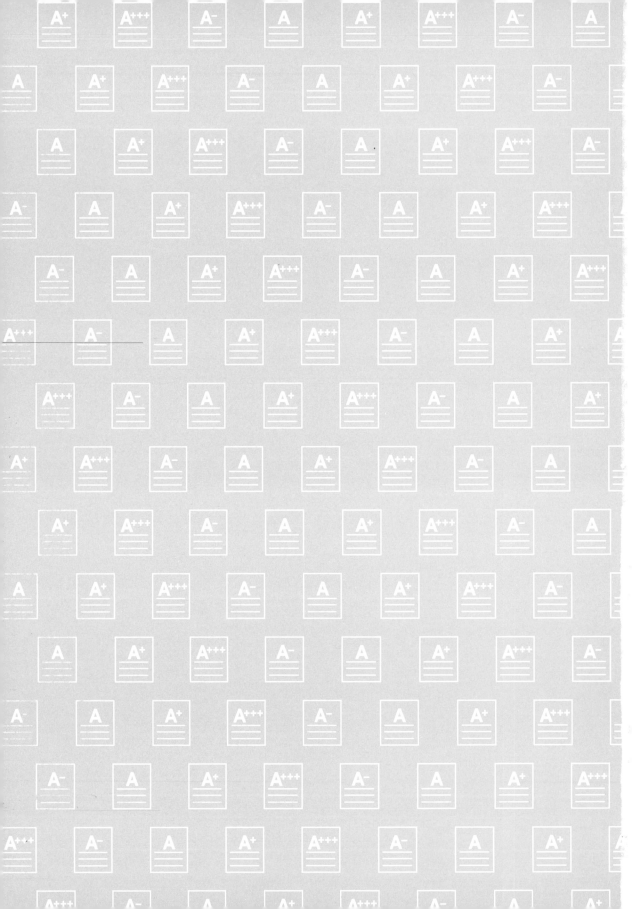

I'M KIND OF
AWESOME

KNOCK
KNOCK®
VENICE, CALIFORNIA

Created and published by Knock Knock
1635-B Electric Ave.
Venice, CA 90291
knockknockstuff.com

ISBN: 978-160106708-1
UPC: 825703-50045-5

10 9 8 7 6

WORD ON THE STREET IS THAT YOU'RE KIND OF
AWESOME
YEAH YOU ARE! TRUE STORY.

But maybe you're doubting? Oh, the doubting. Or maybe you don't doubt your awesomeness (congratulations), but being an awesome person, you know you can't walk down the street proclaiming it unless you want people to give you a lot of space. Whether you're working your way toward awesome and want to record the progress, trying to reclaim your awesomeness after a setback, or looking for a place to revel in awesomeness, this journal will come in handy.

A journal is your safe space to work out your thoughts and ideas in your journey toward awesomeness. It's also where you can celebrate your fantastic feats without anyone throwing shade your way.

The word "awesome" gets tossed around a lot. It's a good idea to remind yourself what it means, so you can decide what kind of awesome you want to be. Here is the definition according to Merriam-Webster:

Causing feelings of fear and wonder : causing feelings of awe : extremely good

1: expressive of awe
2a: inspiring awe
2b: terrific, extraordinary

Most of us are aiming for extremely good, terrific, and/or extraordinary. But no one is saying you can't aim to truly inspire awe. You could even aspire to cause feelings of fear and wonder, particularly if you are an evil genius or the parent of small children.

Are you worried that declaring yourself awesome is not entirely healthy? Don't worry; a soupçon of narcissism isn't bad. Susan Krauss Whitbourne, in her *Psychology Today* article "The Healthy Side of Narcissism," argues that mild narcissism can be good for your well-being. Researchers have called this "adaptive narcissism," which helps people become self-sufficient, self-confident, better at coping with anxiety, and effective leaders. How do you know when you've gone too far? In *O, the Oprah Magazine*, life coach Martha Beck explains how you can differentiate healthy self-esteem from narcissism. "Go to the person in your life who reeks of self-esteem and ask, 'In what ways do you think you need to grow or change?' If the person is psychologically healthy, the list will be as long as your leg. That's because real self-esteem is based on finding areas where we can improve ourselves and honestly working to overcome problems. Healthy people know that they are always a work in progress. Narcissists, on the other hand, will tell you they have nothing to change."

Take a page from Ms. Beck and recognize that self-esteem takes work. Use this journal to record that process and nurture healthy awesomeness.

As noted self-help guru Deepak Chopra claims, "Journaling is one of the most powerful tools we have to transform our lives." In addition to helping put one's mind at ease, journal writing has been shown to aid physical health. According to a widely cited study by James W. Pennebaker and Janel D. Seagal, "Writing about important personal experiences in an emotional way . . . brings about improvements in mental and physical health."

Proven benefits include better stress management, strengthened immune systems, fewer doctor visits, and improvement in chronic illnesses such as asthma. (Sometimes even awesomeness doesn't make it any easier to breathe.)

It's not entirely clear how journaling accomplishes all this. Catharsis is involved, but many also point to the value of organizing experiences into a cohesive narrative. According to *Newsweek*, some experts believe that journaling "forces us to transform the ruminations cluttering our minds into coherent stories." Writing about life can help see where you are growing and changing. In many ways, journaling enables us to see the big picture, so we don't get lost in the small victories and defeats of any given day.

You're no stranger to a journal's value, but how best to use it? Specialists agree that in order to reap the benefits of journaling you have to stick with it, quasi-daily, for as little as five minutes at a time (at least fifteen minutes, however, is best), even on the days when awesomeness seems a distant memory. Finding regular writing times and comfortable locations can help with consistency. If you find yourself unable to muster a single awesome sentiment, don't stress. Instead, use the quotes inside this journal as a jumping-off point for observations and explorations.

What should you write about? The journal is your oyster. Keep track of the ways you want to grow and change. Keep a list of awesome people who you want to emulate, and write about what makes them spectacular. Hold forth on the things you like about yourself. List daily successes, whether success is writing an amazing report or just getting a shower that day. When you do something awkward or stupid, write about that as well. Recognizing and accepting your foibles makes you even more awesome.

Write whatever comes, and don't criticize it; journaling is a means of self-reflection, not a structured composition. In other words, spew. Finally, determine a home for your journal where you can reference it when you're feeling awesome or for that matter, not so awesome.

The great twenty-first century thinker and awesomeness role model Barney Stinson truly knew how to express his greatness: "In my body, where the shame gland should be, there is a second awesome gland." You've got awesome inside of you, too. Embrace and nurture it. So many idiots think they're awesome, but you really kind of are. True story.

And all the colors
I am inside

Have not been
invented yet.

SHEL SILVERSTEIN

DATE		

WHY I'M KIND OF AWESOME TODAY:

_____

_____

_____

_____

_____

_____

_____

_____

_____

_____

_____

_____

_____

_____

_____

_____

_____

_____

_____

_____

_____

_____

_____

_____

MY AWESOMENESS GRADE FOR TODAY:

I'm the most important person in the lives of almost everyone I know and a good number of the people I've never even met.

DAVID SEDARIS

DATE		

WHY I'M KIND OF AWESOME TODAY:

_____

_____

_____

_____

_____

_____

_____

_____

_____

_____

_____

_____

_____

_____

_____

_____

_____

_____

_____

_____

_____

_____

_____

_____

_____

MY AWESOMENESS GRADE FOR TODAY:

I always said I was like those round-bottomed circus dolls—you know, those dolls you could push down and they'd come back up? I've always been like that. I've always said, "No matter what happens, if I get pushed down, I'm going to come right back up."

DORIS DAY

DATE		

WHY I'M KIND OF AWESOME TODAY:

_____

_____

_____

_____

_____

_____

_____

_____

_____

_____

_____

_____

_____

_____

_____

_____

_____

_____

_____

_____

_____

_____

_____

_____

MY AWESOMENESS GRADE FOR TODAY:

I'd always vaguely expected to outgrow my limitations.

GRETCHEN RUBIN

WHY I'M KIND OF AWESOME TODAY:

MY AWESOMENESS GRADE FOR TODAY:

The first time I didn't feel it, but this time I feel it, and I can't deny the fact that you like me, right now, you like me!

SALLY FIELD

WHY I'M KIND OF AWESOME TODAY:

MY AWESOMENESS GRADE FOR TODAY:

I can have oodles of charm when I want to.

KURT VONNEGUT

DATE		

WHY I'M KIND OF AWESOME TODAY:

_____

_____

_____

_____

_____

_____

_____

_____

_____

_____

_____

_____

_____

_____

_____

_____

_____

_____

_____

_____

_____

_____

_____

_____

MY AWESOMENESS GRADE FOR TODAY:

Look at the sky: that is for you. Look at each person's face as you pass on the street: those faces are for you. And the street itself, and the ground under the street, and the ball of fire underneath the ground: all these things are for you.

—————

MIRANDA JULY

WHY I'M KIND OF AWESOME TODAY:

_____

_____

_____

_____

_____

_____

_____

_____

_____

_____

_____

_____

_____

_____

_____

_____

_____

_____

_____

_____

_____

_____

_____

MY AWESOMENESS GRADE FOR TODAY:

Some of us can't help it if we're ravishing.

HARVEY FIERSTEIN

WHY I'M KIND OF AWESOME TODAY:

_____

_____

_____

_____

_____

_____

_____

_____

_____

_____

_____

_____

_____

_____

_____

_____

_____

_____

_____

_____

_____

MY AWESOMENESS GRADE FOR TODAY:

I think I may be the voice of my generation. Or at least a voice of a generation.

DATE		

WHY I'M KIND OF AWESOME TODAY:

_____

_____

_____

_____

_____

_____

_____

_____

_____

_____

_____

_____

_____

_____

_____

_____

_____

_____

_____

_____

_____

_____

_____

_____

_____

_____

_____

MY AWESOMENESS GRADE FOR TODAY:

No need to hurry. No need to sparkle.
No need to be anybody but oneself.

———

VIRGINIA WOOLF

DATE		

WHY I'M KIND OF AWESOME TODAY:

_____

_____

_____

_____

_____

_____

_____

_____

_____

_____

_____

_____

_____

_____

_____

_____

_____

_____

_____

_____

_____

_____

_____

_____

_____

MY AWESOMENESS GRADE FOR TODAY:

It was possible to feel
superior to other people
and like a misfit at the
same time.

JEFFREY EUGENIDES

DATE	

WHY I'M KIND OF AWESOME TODAY:

_____
_____
_____
_____
_____
_____
_____
_____
_____
_____
_____
_____
_____
_____
_____
_____
_____
_____
_____
_____
_____
_____
_____
_____
_____
_____

MY AWESOMENESS GRADE FOR TODAY:

You also have to know what sparks the light in you so that you, in your own way, can illuminate the world.

————————

OPRAH WINFREY

DATE		

WHY I'M KIND OF AWESOME TODAY:

_____

_____

_____

_____

_____

_____

_____

_____

_____

_____

_____

_____

_____

_____

_____

_____

_____

_____

_____

_____

_____

_____

_____

_____

_____

_____

_____

MY AWESOMENESS GRADE FOR TODAY:

I want the title. Not just the money. The title. I'm a champion. I already have money.

ROBERTO DURAN

WHY I'M KIND OF AWESOME TODAY:

MY AWESOMENESS GRADE FOR TODAY:

I'd rather be myself . . . Myself and nasty.
Not somebody else, however jolly.

ALDOUS HUXLEY

DATE		

WHY I'M KIND OF AWESOME TODAY:

_____

_____

_____

_____

_____

_____

_____

_____

_____

_____

_____

_____

_____

_____

_____

_____

_____

_____

_____

_____

_____

_____

_____

_____

_____

_____

MY AWESOMENESS GRADE FOR TODAY:

I am so smart. I am so smart. I am so smart. I am so smart. S-M-R-T—I mean S-M-A-R-T.

HOMER SIMPSON

WHY I'M KIND OF AWESOME TODAY:

_____

_____

_____

_____

_____

_____

_____

_____

_____

_____

_____

_____

_____

_____

_____

_____

_____

_____

_____

_____

_____

_____

_____

_____

_____

_____

_____

MY AWESOMENESS GRADE FOR TODAY:

I personally like being unique. I like being my own person with my own style and my own opinions and my own toothbrush.

ELLEN DEGENERES

DATE

WHY I'M KIND OF AWESOME TODAY:

_____

_____

_____

_____

_____

_____

_____

_____

_____

_____

_____

_____

_____

_____

_____

_____

_____

_____

_____

_____

_____

_____

_____

_____

_____

_____

MY AWESOMENESS GRADE FOR TODAY:

Future hipsters will love me ironically.

MINDY KALING

DATE		

WHY I'M KIND OF AWESOME TODAY:

_____

_____

_____

_____

_____

_____

_____

_____

_____

_____

_____

_____

_____

_____

_____

_____

_____

_____

_____

_____

_____

_____

_____

MY AWESOMENESS GRADE FOR TODAY:

It's like being a little kid again, parading around in a nightgown tucked into your underpants, believing it looks terrific. Your "right mind" knows that you look ridiculous in a half-open dress and giant shoes, but you must put yourself back in third grade, slipping on your mom's quilted caftan and drinking cream soda out of a champagne glass while watching *The Love Boat*. You have never been more glamorous.

TINA FEY

WHY I'M KIND OF AWESOME TODAY:

_____

_____

_____

_____

_____

_____

_____

_____

_____

_____

_____

_____

_____

_____

_____

_____

_____

_____

_____

_____

_____

_____

_____

_____

MY AWESOMENESS GRADE FOR TODAY:

Don't worry where I am. I'll tell you when I get there.

LAWRENCE TAYLOR

WHY I'M KIND OF AWESOME TODAY:

MY AWESOMENESS GRADE FOR TODAY:

If I abstain from fun and such,
I'll probably amount to much;
But I shall stay the way I am,
Because I do not give a damn.

DOROTHY PARKER

DATE

WHY I'M KIND OF AWESOME TODAY:

_____

_____

_____

_____

_____

_____

_____

_____

_____

_____

_____

_____

_____

_____

_____

_____

_____

_____

_____

_____

_____

_____

_____

_____

MY AWESOMENESS GRADE FOR TODAY:

Like a fish which swims calmly in deep water, I felt all about me the secure supporting pressure of my own life. Ragged, inglorious, and apparently purposeless, but my own.

IRIS MURDOCH

DATE

WHY I'M KIND OF AWESOME TODAY:

_____

_____

_____

_____

_____

_____

_____

_____

_____

_____

_____

_____

_____

_____

_____

_____

_____

_____

_____

_____

_____

_____

_____

MY AWESOMENESS GRADE FOR TODAY:

You haven't lived until you've basked in the adoration of the people.

JERRY SPINELLI

	DATE	

WHY I'M KIND OF AWESOME TODAY:

_____

_____

_____

_____

_____

_____

_____

_____

_____

_____

_____

_____

_____

_____

_____

_____

_____

_____

_____

_____

_____

_____

MY AWESOMENESS GRADE FOR TODAY:

I feel pretty / Oh, so pretty / That the city should give me its key / A committee should be organized to honor me.

STEPHEN SONDHEIM

WHY I'M KIND OF AWESOME TODAY:

MY AWESOMENESS GRADE FOR TODAY:

The issue is to accept who you are and revel in that.

MITCH ALBOM

WHY I'M KIND OF AWESOME TODAY:

MY AWESOMENESS GRADE FOR TODAY:

When I was a child, my mother said to me, "If you become a soldier you'll be a general. If you become a monk you'll end up as the Pope." Instead, I became a painter and wound up as Picasso.

PABLO PICASSO

DATE		

WHY I'M KIND OF AWESOME TODAY:

MY AWESOMENESS GRADE FOR TODAY:

Confidence has nothing to do with ability.

AUGUSTEN BURROUGHS

DATE		

WHY I'M KIND OF AWESOME TODAY:

_____

_____

_____

_____

_____

_____

_____

_____

_____

_____

_____

_____

_____

_____

_____

_____

_____

_____

_____

_____

_____

_____

MY AWESOMENESS GRADE FOR TODAY:

Alone had always felt like an actual place to me, as if it weren't a state of being, but rather a room where I could retreat to be who I really was.

_____

CHERYL STRAYED

WHY I'M KIND OF AWESOME TODAY:

MY AWESOMENESS GRADE FOR TODAY:

You your best thing.

TONI MORRISON

DATE	

WHY I'M KIND OF AWESOME TODAY:

_____

_____

_____

_____

_____

_____

_____

_____

_____

_____

_____

_____

_____

_____

_____

_____

_____

_____

_____

_____

_____

_____

_____

MY AWESOMENESS GRADE FOR TODAY:

What I came to realize is that fear, that's the worst of it. That's the real enemy. So, get up, get out in the real world and you kick that bastard as hard you can right in the teeth.

WALTER WHITE (*BREAKING BAD*)

DATE		

WHY I'M KIND OF AWESOME TODAY:

_____

_____

_____

_____

_____

_____

_____

_____

_____

_____

_____

_____

_____

_____

_____

_____

_____

_____

_____

_____

_____

_____

_____

MY AWESOMENESS GRADE FOR TODAY:

I can't afford to spend my time with anyone— there's only enough left for myself.

DANIEL KEYES

DATE

WHY I'M KIND OF AWESOME TODAY:

_____

_____

_____

_____

_____

_____

_____

_____

_____

_____

_____

_____

_____

_____

_____

_____

_____

_____

_____

_____

_____

_____

_____

_____

_____

_____

_____

_____

MY AWESOMENESS GRADE FOR TODAY:

I was someone with not much self-belief at all and yet in this one thing in my life I believed. That was the one thing in my life. I felt "I can tell a story."

J. K. ROWLING

WHY I'M KIND OF AWESOME TODAY:

_____

_____

_____

_____

_____

_____

_____

_____

_____

_____

_____

_____

_____

_____

_____

_____

_____

_____

_____

_____

_____

_____

_____

_____

_____

_____

_____

MY AWESOMENESS GRADE FOR TODAY:

Insult my sexual prowess, my intellect, but not my pancakes.

MOBY

DATE		

WHY I'M KIND OF AWESOME TODAY:

_____

_____

_____

_____

_____

_____

_____

_____

_____

_____

_____

_____

_____

_____

_____

_____

_____

_____

_____

_____

_____

_____

_____

_____

MY AWESOMENESS GRADE FOR TODAY:

I'm young and strong, there isn't anything I can't do.

ANN PETRY

WHY I'M KIND OF AWESOME TODAY:

MY AWESOMENESS GRADE FOR TODAY:

Off the pillow and into the air / I'm ready
'cause it's my day / Situation: it's all
possible / Everything is going my way.

———
LE TIGRE

DATE		

WHY I'M KIND OF AWESOME TODAY:

_____

_____

_____

_____

_____

_____

_____

_____

_____

_____

_____

_____

_____

_____

_____

_____

_____

_____

_____

_____

_____

_____

_____

_____

_____

MY AWESOMENESS GRADE FOR TODAY:

Your true being is connected to all that exists.

DEEPAK CHOPRA

DATE		

WHY I'M KIND OF AWESOME TODAY:

_____

_____

_____

_____

_____

_____

_____

_____

_____

_____

_____

_____

_____

_____

_____

_____

_____

_____

_____

_____

_____

_____

_____

_____

_____

_____

_____

_____

MY AWESOMENESS GRADE FOR TODAY:

Once I had asked God for one or two extra inches in height, but instead he made me as tall as the sky, so high that I could not measure myself.

MALALA YOUSAFZAI

WHY I'M KIND OF AWESOME TODAY:

MY AWESOMENESS GRADE FOR TODAY:

There's not a thing wrong with you, you're right all the way through.

EMMA DONOGHUE

DATE	

WHY I'M KIND OF AWESOME TODAY:

MY AWESOMENESS GRADE FOR TODAY:

I don't want anybody telling me
what I'm supposed to look like.
Or tell me that I'm wrong because
I look a certain way. Or not the way
they think I should be looking.

WHOOPI GOLDBERG

DATE

WHY I'M KIND OF AWESOME TODAY:

_____

_____

_____

_____

_____

_____

_____

_____

_____

_____

_____

_____

_____

_____

_____

_____

_____

_____

_____

_____

_____

_____

_____

_____

_____

_____

_____

MY AWESOMENESS GRADE FOR TODAY:

Everyone is in me, and I am a part of everyone.

JAMES FRANCO

WHY I'M KIND OF AWESOME TODAY:

_____

_____

_____

_____

_____

_____

_____

_____

_____

_____

_____

_____

_____

_____

_____

_____

_____

_____

_____

_____

_____

_____

_____

_____

_____

MY AWESOMENESS GRADE FOR TODAY:

I discovered at a very early age that if I talk long enough, I can make anything right or wrong.

DAN HARMON

WHY I'M KIND OF AWESOME TODAY:

_____

_____

_____

_____

_____

_____

_____

_____

_____

_____

_____

_____

_____

_____

_____

_____

_____

_____

_____

_____

_____

_____

_____

_____

_____

MY AWESOMENESS GRADE FOR TODAY:

I'm me, and I like that there are people who have an appreciation for that.

ZOOEY DESCHANEL

WHY I'M KIND OF AWESOME TODAY:

_____

_____

_____

_____

_____

_____

_____

_____

_____

_____

_____

_____

_____

_____

_____

_____

_____

_____

_____

_____

_____

_____

_____

_____

_____

MY AWESOMENESS GRADE FOR TODAY:

I didn't ask to be born hot.

JA'MIE KING

WHY I'M KIND OF AWESOME TODAY:

_____

_____

_____

_____

_____

_____

_____

_____

_____

_____

_____

_____

_____

_____

_____

_____

_____

_____

_____

_____

_____

MY AWESOMENESS GRADE FOR TODAY:

I'm working on my own life story.
I don't mean I'm putting it together;
no, I'm taking it apart.

MARGARET ATWOOD

DATE		

WHY I'M KIND OF AWESOME TODAY:

_____

_____

_____

_____

_____

_____

_____

_____

_____

_____

_____

_____

_____

_____

_____

_____

_____

_____

_____

_____

_____

_____

MY AWESOMENESS GRADE FOR TODAY:

The man who does not value himself, cannot value anything or anyone.

AYN RAND

DATE	

WHY I'M KIND OF AWESOME TODAY:

_____

_____

_____

_____

_____

_____

_____

_____

_____

_____

_____

_____

_____

_____

_____

_____

_____

_____

_____

_____

_____

_____

_____

_____

_____

_____

_____

MY AWESOMENESS GRADE FOR TODAY:

I am the only person in the world I should like to know thoroughly.

OSCAR WILDE

DATE		

WHY I'M KIND OF AWESOME TODAY:

_____

_____

_____

_____

_____

_____

_____

_____

_____

_____

_____

_____

_____

_____

_____

_____

_____

_____

_____

_____

_____

_____

_____

MY AWESOMENESS GRADE FOR TODAY:

Helped are those who are content to be themselves; they will never lack mystery in their lives and the joys of self-discovery will be constant.

ALICE WALKER

DATE		

WHY I'M KIND OF AWESOME TODAY:

MY AWESOMENESS GRADE FOR TODAY:

All I know is that I'm going to do whatever makes me feel comfortable, and I'm gonna do whatever I want to do and hope that the essence of me and what people liked about me in the beginning will come through.

TIG NOTARO

DATE

WHY I'M KIND OF AWESOME TODAY:

MY AWESOMENESS GRADE FOR TODAY:

I've done it all, and
I've loved every
trashy minute of it.

JOHN WATERS

DATE

WHY I'M KIND OF AWESOME TODAY:

_____

_____

_____

_____

_____

_____

_____

_____

_____

_____

_____

_____

_____

_____

_____

_____

_____

_____

_____

_____

_____

_____

_____

_____

_____

_____

MY AWESOMENESS GRADE FOR TODAY:

Every day, I define myself. I know who I am today. I don't promise you anything for tomorrow.

SALMA HAYEK

DATE		

WHY I'M KIND OF AWESOME TODAY:

_____

_____

_____

_____

_____

_____

_____

_____

_____

_____

_____

_____

_____

_____

_____

_____

_____

_____

_____

_____

_____

_____

_____

_____

MY AWESOMENESS GRADE FOR TODAY:

Does my sexiness upset you?
Does it come as a surprise
That I dance like I've got diamonds
At the meeting of my thighs?

MAYA ANGELOU

DATE		

WHY I'M KIND OF AWESOME TODAY:

MY AWESOMENESS GRADE FOR TODAY:

We do what we do, because of who we are. If we did otherwise, we would not be ourselves.

NEIL GAIMAN

WHY I'M KIND OF AWESOME TODAY:

MY AWESOMENESS GRADE FOR TODAY:

Dressing badly has been a refuge much of my life, a way of compelling others to engage with my mind, not my physical presence.

SONIA SOTOMAYOR

WHY I'M KIND OF AWESOME TODAY:

_____

_____

_____

_____

_____

_____

_____

_____

_____

_____

_____

_____

_____

_____

_____

_____

_____

_____

_____

_____

_____

_____

_____

_____

MY AWESOMENESS GRADE FOR TODAY:

I can be
me. I can
be whoever
because I'm
true to me.

TUPAC SHAKUR

DATE		

WHY I'M KIND OF AWESOME TODAY:

_____

_____

_____

_____

_____

_____

_____

_____

_____

_____

_____

_____

_____

_____

_____

_____

_____

_____

_____

_____

_____

_____

_____

_____

_____

_____

_____

_____

_____

_____

MY AWESOMENESS GRADE FOR TODAY:

Don't you ever let a person make you feel bad because you love something they decided is only for nerds. You're loving a thing that's for you.

WIL WHEATON

WHY I'M KIND OF AWESOME TODAY:

_____

_____

_____

_____

_____

_____

_____

_____

_____

_____

_____

_____

_____

_____

_____

_____

_____

_____

_____

_____

_____

_____

MY AWESOMENESS GRADE FOR TODAY:

I'm a fountain of blood /
In the shape of a girl.

BJÖRK

DATE		

WHY I'M KIND OF AWESOME TODAY:

MY AWESOMENESS GRADE FOR TODAY:

Follow your inner moonlight; don't hide the madness.

ALLEN GINSBERG

WHY I'M KIND OF AWESOME TODAY:

MY AWESOMENESS GRADE FOR TODAY:

When I am in my painting, I'm not aware of what I'm doing . . . I have no fears about making changes, destroying the image, etc., because the painting has a life of its own.

JACKSON POLLOCK

WHY I'M KIND OF AWESOME TODAY:

_____

_____

_____

_____

_____

_____

_____

_____

_____

_____

_____

_____

_____

_____

_____

_____

_____

_____

_____

_____

_____

_____

_____

_____

_____

MY AWESOMENESS GRADE FOR TODAY:

You want me down on Earth / But I am up in space.

— **ICONA POP**

WHY I'M KIND OF AWESOME TODAY:

MY AWESOMENESS GRADE FOR TODAY:

A strong sense of identity gives man an idea he can do no wrong; too little accomplishes the same.

DJUNA BARNES

WHY I'M KIND OF AWESOME TODAY:

MY AWESOMENESS GRADE FOR TODAY:

I am who I am, doing
what I came to do.
———
AUDRE LORDE

WHY I'M KIND OF AWESOME TODAY:

MY AWESOMENESS GRADE FOR TODAY:

Picture you talking to your own daughter, or your younger sister—because you would tell your younger sister or your daughter that she was beautiful, and you wouldn't be lying. Because she is. And so are you.

AMY POEHLER

DATE		

WHY I'M KIND OF AWESOME TODAY:

_____

_____

_____

_____

_____

_____

_____

_____

_____

_____

_____

_____

_____

_____

_____

_____

_____

_____

_____

_____

_____

_____

_____

_____

_____

_____

_____

MY AWESOMENESS GRADE FOR TODAY:

I'm just an advertisement /
For a version of myself.

DAVID BYRNE

DATE		

WHY I'M KIND OF AWESOME TODAY:

_____

_____

_____

_____

_____

_____

_____

_____

_____

_____

_____

_____

_____

_____

_____

_____

_____

_____

_____

_____

_____

_____

_____

_____

_____

_____

_____

MY AWESOMENESS GRADE FOR TODAY:

I got their attention, I got their approval, their admiration, their approbation, and their applause. And those are the only A's I wanted, and I got 'em.

———

GEORGE CARLIN

WHY I'M KIND OF AWESOME TODAY:

MY AWESOMENESS GRADE FOR TODAY:

The universe and the
light of the stars
come through me.

I am the crescent
moon put up over the
gate to the festival.

—
RUMI

DATE		

WHY I'M KIND OF AWESOME TODAY:

_____

_____

_____

_____

_____

_____

_____

_____

_____

_____

_____

_____

_____

_____

_____

_____

_____

_____

_____

_____

_____

_____

_____

_____

_____

_____

MY AWESOMENESS GRADE FOR TODAY:

I am a champion /
And you're gonna
hear me roar.

KATY PERRY

DATE

WHY I'M KIND OF AWESOME TODAY:

_____

_____

_____

_____

_____

_____

_____

_____

_____

_____

_____

_____

_____

_____

_____

_____

_____

_____

_____

_____

_____

_____

_____

_____

_____

_____

_____

_____

_____

MY AWESOMENESS GRADE FOR TODAY:

I'm eighty years old and I'm twerking.

JOAN RIVERS

DATE		

WHY I'M KIND OF AWESOME TODAY:

_____

_____

_____

_____

_____

_____

_____

_____

_____

_____

_____

_____

_____

_____

_____

_____

_____

_____

_____

_____

_____

_____

_____

_____

MY AWESOMENESS GRADE FOR TODAY:

I think I'll try
defying gravity /
And you can't pull
me down.

STEPHEN SCHWARTZ

WHY I'M KIND OF AWESOME TODAY:

_____

_____

_____

_____

_____

_____

_____

_____

_____

_____

_____

_____

_____

_____

_____

_____

_____

_____

_____

_____

_____

_____

_____

_____

MY AWESOMENESS GRADE FOR TODAY:

Don't call me crazy. I'm a survivor. I do what I have to do to survive.

STIEG LARSSON

DATE		

WHY I'M KIND OF AWESOME TODAY:

MY AWESOMENESS GRADE FOR TODAY:

I'm not going to censor myself to comfort your ignorance.

JON STEWART

DATE		

WHY I'M KIND OF AWESOME TODAY:

_____

_____

_____

_____

_____

_____

_____

_____

_____

_____

_____

_____

_____

_____

_____

_____

_____

_____

_____

_____

_____

_____

_____

MY AWESOMENESS GRADE FOR TODAY:

You need not apologize for being brilliant, talented, gorgeous, rich, or smart.

MARIANNE WILLIAMSON

DATE		

WHY I'M KIND OF AWESOME TODAY:

_____

_____

_____

_____

_____

_____

_____

_____

_____

_____

_____

_____

_____

_____

_____

_____

_____

_____

_____

_____

_____

_____

_____

MY AWESOMENESS GRADE FOR TODAY:

Besides,
They'll see how
    beautiful I am
And be ashamed—
I, too, am America.

LANGSTON HUGHES

DATE		

WHY I'M KIND OF AWESOME TODAY:

_____

_____

_____

_____

_____

_____

_____

_____

_____

_____

_____

_____

_____

_____

_____

_____

_____

_____

_____

_____

_____

_____

_____

_____

_____

_____

_____

_____

_____

_____

MY AWESOMENESS GRADE FOR TODAY:

We begin to find and become ourselves when we notice how we are already found, already truly, entirely, wildly, messily, marvelously who we were born to be.

ANNE LAMOTT

DATE		

WHY I'M KIND OF AWESOME TODAY:

_____

_____

_____

_____

_____

_____

_____

_____

_____

_____

_____

_____

_____

_____

_____

_____

_____

_____

_____

_____

_____

_____

_____

_____

_____

MY AWESOMENESS GRADE FOR TODAY:

I celebrate myself, and sing myself,
And what I assume you shall assume,
For every atom belonging to me as
good belongs to you.

WALT WHITMAN

WHY I'M KIND OF AWESOME TODAY:

_____

_____

_____

_____

_____

_____

_____

_____

_____

_____

_____

_____

_____

_____

_____

_____

_____

_____

_____

_____

_____

_____

MY AWESOMENESS GRADE FOR TODAY:

I am a leaf on the wind, watch how I soar.

KEITH R. A. DECANDIDO

DATE		

WHY I'M KIND OF AWESOME TODAY:

MY AWESOMENESS GRADE FOR TODAY:

After all, what nobler thought can one cherish than that the universe lives within us all?

———————

NEIL DEGRASSE TYSON

	DATE	

WHY I'M KIND OF AWESOME TODAY:

_____

_____

_____

_____

_____

_____

_____

_____

_____

_____

_____

_____

_____

_____

_____

_____

_____

_____

_____

_____

_____

_____

_____

_____

_____

_____

_____

MY AWESOMENESS GRADE FOR TODAY:

Nothing is accomplished without
making fools of ourselves.

GLORIA STEINEM

WHY I'M KIND OF AWESOME TODAY:

MY AWESOMENESS GRADE FOR TODAY:

This is the fast lane, folks . . . and some of us like it here.

HUNTER S. THOMPSON

DATE

WHY I'M KIND OF AWESOME TODAY:

_____

_____

_____

_____

_____

_____

_____

_____

_____

_____

_____

_____

_____

_____

_____

_____

_____

_____

_____

_____

_____

_____

_____

MY AWESOMENESS GRADE FOR TODAY:

Yup, you rule.

———

KNOCK KNOCK